The Sun
Our Amazing Star

by Patricia Brennan Demuth

Grosset & Dunlap
An Imprint of Penguin Random House

For Liz Perry, a bright beam of sunshine—PBD

GROSSET & DUNLAP
Penguin Young Readers Group
An Imprint of Penguin Random House LLC

Photo credits: front cover: © NASA; back cover: (background) © Thinkstock/Natalia_80, (sun) © Thinkstock/DigtialStorm; page 1: © Thinkstock/DigtialStorm; page 3: © Thinkstock/ standret; pages 4–5: © Thinkstock/Vladmax; page 6: © Thinkstock/Stocktrek Images; page 9: © NASA/SDO; page 10: © Thinkstock/muratart; pages 12–13: © Thinkstock/LUNAMARINA; pages 14–15: (trees) © Thinkstock/Ryan McVay, (sun art) © Thinkstock/sumkinn; page 17: © Thinkstock/Mike Watson Images; page 18: © Thinkstock/Jupiterimages; page 19: © Thinkstock/altrendo images; pages 20–21: © Thinkstock/VladislavStarozhilov; pages 22–23: © Thinkstock/Chris Harvey; pages 24–25: © Thinkstock/Comstock; page 26: © Thinkstock/Johannes Gerhardus Swanepoel; page 29: © NASA/SDO; pages 30–31: © Thinkstock/solarseven; page 32: © Thinkstock/Zurijeta.

Library of Congress Cataloging-in-Publication Data is available.

ISBN 9780448488288   10 9 8 7 6 5 4 3

At night,
you can see stars
shining brightly.
But did you know that
you can see one star shining
during the day?

Our Sun!
That's right.
The Sun is a star.
Billions of stars fill the universe.
Is the Sun the biggest star of all?

No.
It just looks that way because the Sun
is the closest star to Earth.

The Sun is much, MUCH bigger
than Earth.
One million Earths
could fit inside the Sun.
The Earth is solid.
You can walk on it.
But the Sun is a ball of burning gas.
Gas is like air.
It doesn't hold its shape.

In photos taken from space,
the Sun looks like it's boiling.
The bubbling gases are HOT—
sizzling hot!
If a spaceship got too close,
the Sun would melt it apart.

Gases inside the Sun
EXPLODE every second,
like bombs.
Wham! Bam!
Scientists say the Sun is very loud!

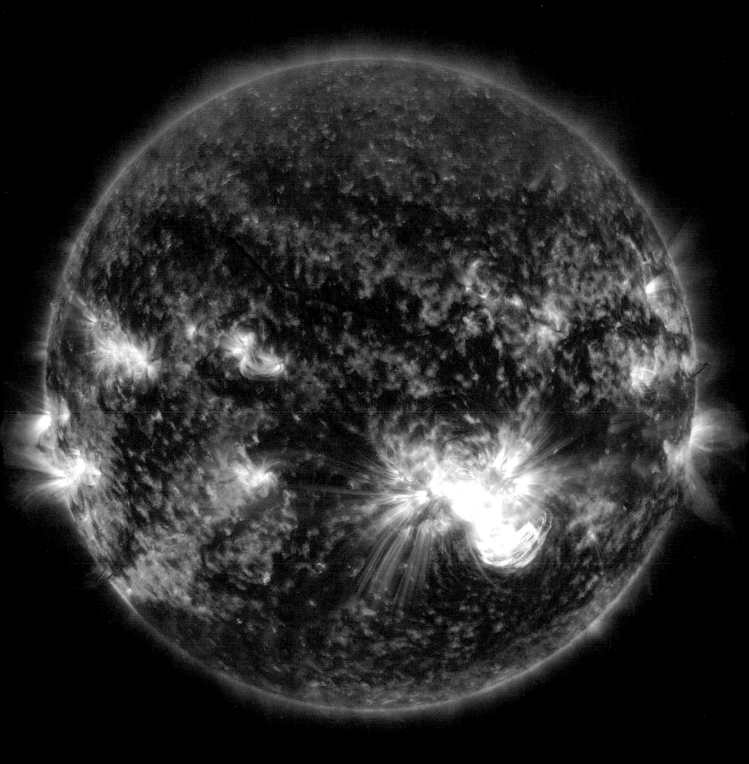

The Sun's gas bombs
shoot out heat and light.
The heat and light travel to Earth—
ninety-three million miles away!
The fastest airplane
would take eighteen years to go that far.
But Sun rays reach Earth in just eight minutes!

Sun rays bring life to our planet.
Imagine Earth without the Sun's heat and light.
It would be dark,
cold,
and dead.
Nothing could live.
Nothing at all.

The Sun feeds our plants
so our plants can feed us.
Leaves soak in energy from sunlight.
Plants mix the sunlight
with air and water
to make a special sugar.
The sugar keeps plants alive.
The plants keep animals alive.
And animals and plants keep us alive.

Your skin soaks in sunlight, too,
just like the leaves of plants.
Your body turns
the Sun's energy
into vitamin D.
This "sunshine vitamin"
makes bones strong.

But too much sunlight
can be harmful.
That's why
you need sunscreen.

Today we can trap the Sun's energy
and use it for power.
We call it **solar energy**.
It's the same energy that dries
wet clothes outdoors.

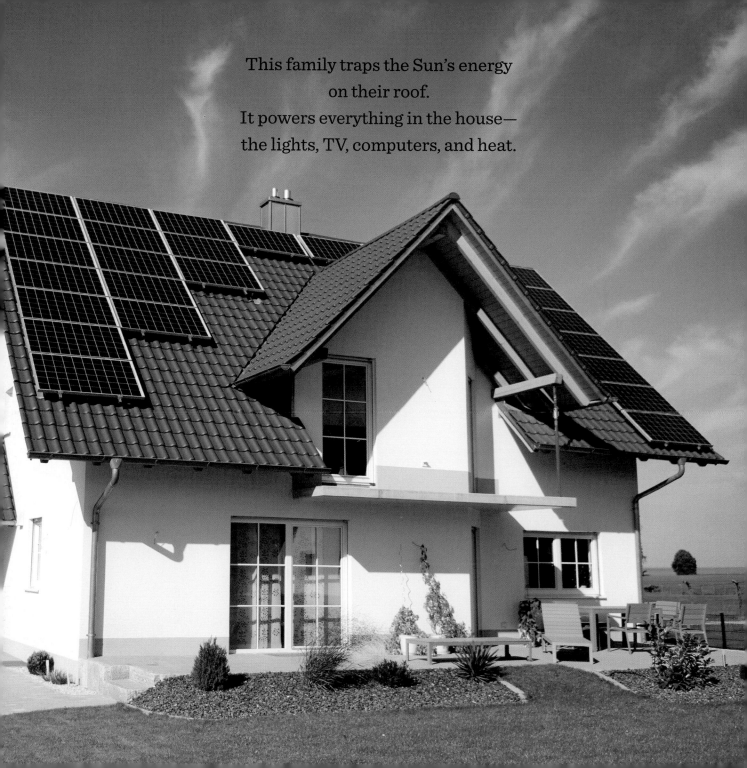

This family traps the Sun's energy
on their roof.
It powers everything in the house—
the lights, TV, computers, and heat.

The Sun powers our cars, too.
How can that be?
Gas and oil come from plants
that lived long, long ago.
When the plants died,
they were covered
by dirt and rock.

Millions of years passed.
The buried plants decayed in many stages.
Finally, they turned into fuels.
The Sun's energy
from the ancient plants
was still stored inside!

The Sun never stops shining.
But at night, its light disappears.
That's because the Earth spins.
Each spin of the Earth
takes twenty-four hours.
We have day when
our side of Earth faces the Sun.
We have night when
we face away from the Sun.

Hot, sunny days
come from the Sun,
of course.
But so do rainy days!
That's because rain starts with heat.

The Sun heats up our waters—
lakes, rivers, and oceans.
The top of the water turns into **vapor**—
a gas made of tiny raindrops.
The vapor rises in the air
and becomes a cloud.
Later the rain falls.

Today we know a lot about the Sun.
Scientists can send satellites into space.
These machines
have telescopes and cameras inside.
They can take
close-up photos of the Sun,
even from far away.

Right this minute,
many satellites are circling in space.
They send back amazing photos
of the Sun.

In this photo,
fiery gas shoots out
from the Sun.
It's called a **solar flare**.
Some solar flares are bigger than Earth!

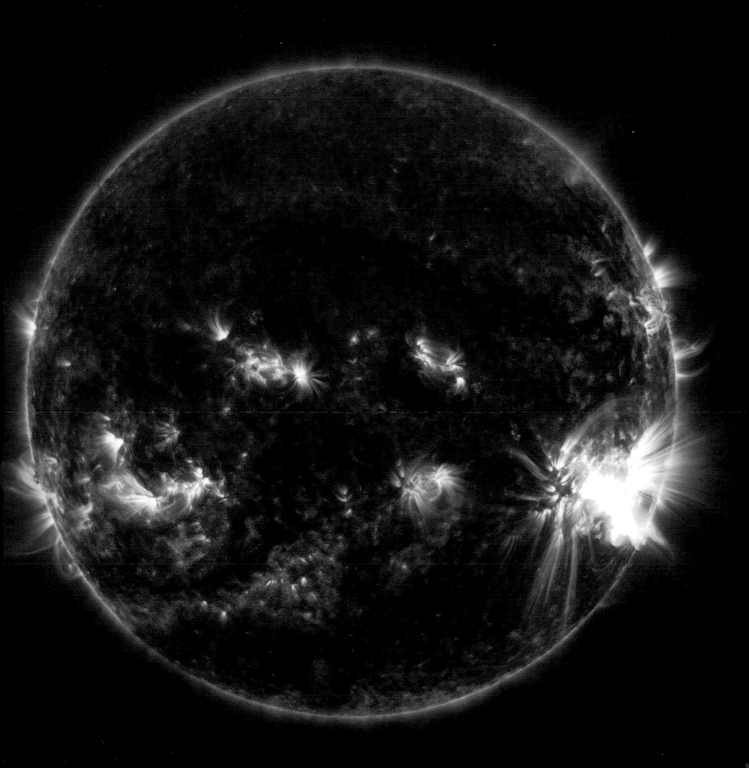

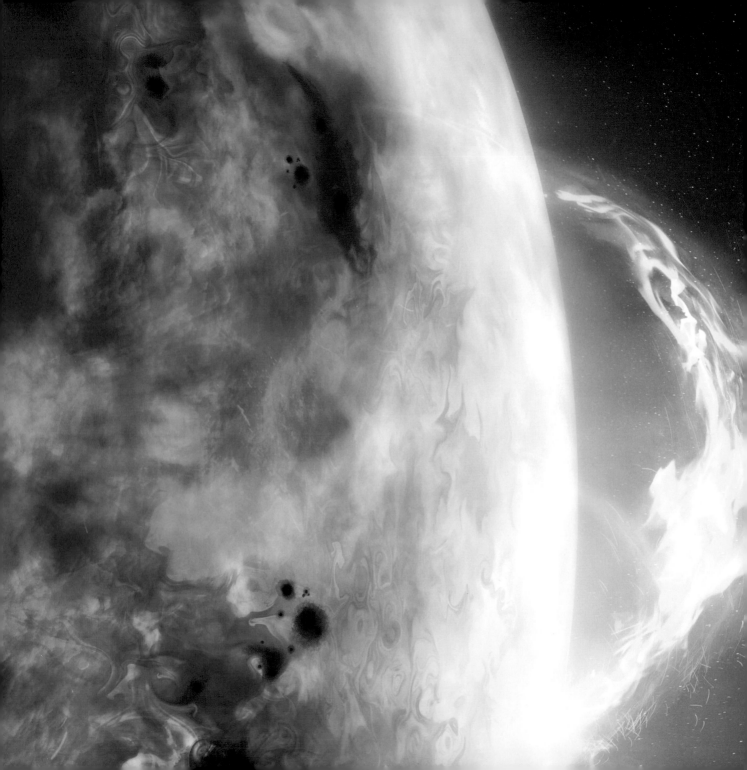

Here giant flames
leap from the Sun
and loop back.
These loops of gas
can last for months.

The Sun is just one star in the universe.
But it's *our* star—
the most important one of all.